# *Brew* U

## by Justine Shearstone

*Brew* a new idea within **U** and perk up your life!

*Brew* **U**

Brew U by Justine Joy Shearstone

Books may be purchased in quantity by contacting ShearstoneMedia@hotmail.com.

Published by: Shearstone Media
Cover Design: Shearstone Media

ISBN 978-0-692-29813-8

First Edition, 2014
Printed in the United States of America

www.justineshearstone.com

*Brew* **U**

*For my Mother, Rose Ann Herl, who taught me compassion, courage, integrity, dedication, love and to always BREW with God in mind and heart.*

*Brew* **U**

## Table of *Contents*

# Brew U

# *Brew* U

# *Brew* **U**

# *Brew* U

### Are You Living in High Definition?

TV enthusiasts know what it means to watch something in high definition. The picture is crystal clear. The images are almost life-like. You feel like you are a part of the action. When the broadcast world switched to high definition and audiences started buying HD TV's and abandoning their old standard definition TV's, the picture quality was extremely noticeable. And people love it.

Recently, I noticed some high definition versus standard definition in my new prescription contacts. In my left eye, things were crystal clear: high definition! In my right eye, it was more standard definition. Good picture, but not fantastic. As I was sitting and waiting for him to examine me, I began to **BREW** about how important my eyesight was to me (and not just because I used to work in television video production). I realized how quickly I was bothered by the idea that I could not see in "high definition" in both eyes and how eager I was to get it fixed. From that point on, I knew I would never take my eyesight for granted.

Are there some things in your life that *U* take for granted? How will *U* preserve those things that are truly important to *U*?

## Baker's Dozen

I can't bake a pie. And this weekend, I learned I can't bake a quiche either.

Today, I find myself slowly accepting defeat and ***BREW***ing on my strengths. I can bake a cake. I can make a great chicken dish. I need to remember that God gave me certain skills to shine that are different from other people. This way I can work together uniquely with other people and their talents for His purpose. So, I have assembled my own "baker's dozen" and am focused on things that I feel confident in:

1. I am responsible

2. I am a good friend

3. I am courteous and kind

4. I value my family and my moral integrity

5. I can cook

6. I am severely organized

7. I am reliable

8. I am making positive changes in my life

9. I laugh at my own jokes

# *Brew* **U**

10. I am sincere

11. I am generous when I can be

12. I am complimentary

13. I can bring a dessert to your next gathering – just don't ask me to bake a pie!

What are your baker's dozen? Your ingredients that bake you into who **U** are?

*Brew* **U**

Comment Cards

During my recent trip to Ohio to visit family, I encountered many people who took their jobs seriously, put customer needs first, and most of all, kept a friendly disposition in the process of a cancelled flight. It was a breath of fresh air to be honest. In this day and age where so many people are buried in their smart phones, on edge because of personal problems, or just plain disgruntled, going to and fro in public places can be a real drag!

As most of you know, I am a strong advocate of comment cards, comment calls, or comment emails. Not for negative feedback, but for positive ones. I personally think a kind word goes a long way. I know I appreciate positive comments that are written about me. During this flight cancellation experience, I ***BREW***ed over how I was going to contact each company to report my positive feedback and express my sincere gratitude for their individual employee's service. I've just finished submitting my comments.

When was the last time *U* filled out a comment card – or expressed your appreciation for a person or business?

# *Brew* **U**

## Daylight Sharing Time

I have travelled by car and plane by myself countless times, but for the first time, I recently vacationed alone (well, somewhat). I met up with an old friend in Las Vegas who was there for work, so we had limited time together in the evenings. My daylight hours were spent on the Vegas Strip, wandering in and out of casinos, shopping cubbies, and restaurants.

The experience was eye-opening:
1.  I had never been to Vegas. The buildings, the people, and the attractions were sights to behold.
2. I had plenty of time to take in the things that I was truly interested in. I didn't have to worry about lingering too long.
3. Then there's the convenience of getting around. Being alone, you can easily squeeze in and out of crowds and don't have to worry about making sure your group is still intact.

I am glad I did it. But as I ***BREW*** about this, I am not sure if I want to do it again. Like I mentioned, a few hours each evening were spent with my old friend, but in the future, I think I prefer to have Daylight Sharing Time, too.

Have *U* ever vacationed alone? Did *U* enjoy it?

*Brew* **U**

## EnterTAMEment

How do *U* define the word, "entertainment"?

I was recently involved in a discussion around this word and everyone seemed to have a different opinion as to what it meant. Here are some of the answers that were given:

1. Entertainment = "…doing something I enjoy doing." This person felt entertainment was your own perception of it.

2. Entertainment = "Celebrities and the like." A side note to my former colleagues in the TV industry – this type of entertainment got a thumb's down, since it seemed that "entertainment" was taking over TV news.

3. Entertainment = Facebook, social media, computerized and handheld gadgets, etc.

A few hours later, I heard an evangelist give her own spin on entertainment. She said some people tend to put entertainment first over God and that we should be taming those activities and putting Him first.

I began to **BREW** over that exact thought and that is where I came up with the phrase "enterTAMEment." Do *U* need to tame your entertainment?

*Brew* **U**

## Fall Classics

Fall is in the air. You wouldn't know it if you stepped outside my window, though. As I write this, it is 85 degrees and not yet noon in Southwest Florida.

But I don't let my current circumstances block out my Ohio childhood. My brother's birthday is just around the corner. I fondly remember my Grandma baking a cake for him when we were kids and adorning it with those tri-colored candy corns and candy pumpkins, one of those classic symbols of the fall season. This week I began to **BREW** over this (like I do every year) when I popped his birthday card in the mail. I always pause and smile and think of those candy pumpkins laced in frosting.

Then there are other fall classics. I remember us watching "The Great Pumpkin, Charlie Brown" every year in my parent's living room. My favorite part is when Sally has her meltdown with Linus in the pumpkin patch and rages about missing out "on tricks or treats" which is still quoted among my close inner circle of friends. Then there's the apple cider donuts, the gorgeous fall leaves in my parent's backyard, pulling out the sweaters, etc.

How about *U*? What are some of your "fall classics"?

# *Brew* **U**

## "Good" Bye

Some people hate goodbyes. So much so that they refuse to even say the word. They opt for "See you later" or "Until next time" no matter how long the time may be in between visits.

While sometimes goodbye can be seen as a negative, I see it as a GOOD thing. No, not the "goodbye and good riddance" idea, but rather as time well spent.

"Good"-bye to me is:

• Wishing the other "good" things as time carries on
• An appreciation for having had the opportunity to know or spend time with them, whether it's for a Moment or for several years

The "Good" byes have been **BREW**ing a lot lately as I prepare to say goodbye to dear ones before moving out of state. While I may not be as easily accessible in person, I am not going anywhere in mind, spirit, and heart. And that, I believe, is a GOOD thing!

What does the word goodbye mean to *U*?

# *Brew* U

Hidden Sweet Treats

After watching a segment on the local news, I felt compelled to visit Bangor-based chocolate shop, Specialty Sweets.

The store was lined down the middle and on all sides with all sorts of truffles, fudge, and chocolates. On the opposite side, you can find sugary delights such as licorice, gummies, and hard candies. And in the back, gelato.

Clearly, this was a place for those with a sweet tooth. But what made the visit even sweeter were the owners. As I toured the place, I noticed Christian music playing on the radio and I watched as the people behind the counter treated customers with kindness, respect, and dare I say it, the sweetest smiles.

I struck up a conversation with the owners themselves and found them to be delightful. They are a young couple who devote their mornings and nights to their chocolate shop.

As the discussion progressed, I began to **BREW**. I originally stopped in for the sugary products, but to see young, Christian-based business owners so devoted, pleasant, kind, and hardworking was the real sweet treat for me. I have since returned and will continue to do so.

What about *U*: what businesses or business owners are sweet treats for *U*?

*Brew* **U**

Inside the Owner's Box

Exotic food, elaborate drinks, oversized cushion chairs, big screen televisions, fame, fortune – just some of the adjectives mentioned when you ask sports fans to describe "The Owner's Box."

While watching a special on ESPN, celebrities and fans alike were explaining what they witnessed and experienced while sitting in one NFL Owner's Box. The people interviewed said they were welcomed like family with genuine smiles, warm handshakes, laughter, and an overall sense of belonging for those few precious hours while watching their favorite team play.

They were there to watch the game but the game itself seemed to be the side attraction.  While watching with the owner in the "Owner's Box" is truly an honor,  it was the feeling, the attention to detail, and the special acknowledgement received just for being there that seemed to be the main event. A place that was remote, yet warm and welcoming.

 This got me ***BREW****ing. While I will never probably sit in an NFL Owner's Box, I know of some places that are just as wonderful and welcoming: the homes of family and friends. These are by far the best of the best when it comes to the "Owner's Box."

Do *U* have an "Owner's Box" that *U* visit? What is it about that place that makes it so special?

# *Brew* **U**

Jan-U-ary

Do you make resolutions? I have been known to adopt some but I don't like to call them "resolutions" because of the negative connotations that can be associated with the word.

I often say I am making "changes." Changes in the way I approach finances. Changes in the way I eat each day. Changes in the amount of water I drink daily, you get the idea.

However, this year my normal approach to change is, well, changing. Instead, I am thankful for the things that have NOT changed: the things that remain constant in my life. I appreciate those involved in my health. I am extremely grateful for my husband, along with my current family, for their unchanging love and support no matter what the situation. The loyalty of my friends also remains intact.

And that has me ***BREW***ing – what are some of the things that *U* wouldn't want changed? What are the constants in your life that deserve to be highlighted?

*Brew* **U**

## Killin' It with Kindness

As I write this, it is the dead of winter. But in the midst of the cold and show, I experienced some real warmth during a recent visit from Bangor, Maine to Erie, PA.

Upon flying into Erie, our plane was diverted to Buffalo, NY due to a massive blizzard. The 30 or so passengers and I were instructed to wait for a tour bus that was going to drive us to Erie. (I was hesitant of this considering we were actually going to be driving into the blizzard.) Surprisingly, this group was quiet and kept frustrations hidden. We all exited the plane and headed to the baggage claim to grab our luggage and find the bus.

In an instant, it felt as though we were family. The airline wasn't exactly the most communicative, so whenever one passenger got news of something they immediately shared it with the group.

The normal 2 hour bus ride turned into almost 6. At one point the bus came to a standstill for nearly 2 hours after authorities closed the highway because of the storm. Still, no one raised their voice or demonstrated any frustration or angst. Everyone even thanked the bus driver!

I *BREW* about this is because I was amazed at how everyone was calm, relaxed, and most of all kind to each other. It was then that I realized that we all were killin' it (frustrations, anger, angst, inconvenience) with kindness.

Are there things that *U* can kill with kindness?

# *Brew* **U**

## Let Me See Your Teeth

Today, I received a picture of myself in the mail and I was smiling. This is actually unusual for me!

Later in the day, with the photo on my mind, I stopped into a store and noticed that no one there was smiling. In fact, there was one woman there who clearly looked like she was having a rough day. So, I did the unusual: I flashed her a smile. Surprisingly, her face lit up and she flashed one back. I am hoping this little gesture was a bright spot for her on what appeared to be a cloudy day.

I got to **BREW**ing about this silent exchange. We tend to coat emails, texts, even Facebook statuses and Twitter posts with smiley faces. Yet, how many of us actually physically smile to each other each day? Do we tend to type this emotion more than we actually show it? We probably need to demonstrate it now more than ever with all that is going on in our world.

On that note – I am daring myself – and *U* – to try and smile more in general and to especially flash a smile at strangers.

*U* never know – your pearly whites could be just what someone needs on an otherwise tarnished day.

*Brew* **U**

## Melodious Memories

Often times we hear the phrase, "The power of the spoken word." But I feel that "the power of a song" can be just as, well, powerful.

Today, I heard a song that quickly transported me back in time. I remember exactly where I first heard it. I remember who I was with. I even remember the surroundings and the smells. As the song ended, I began to think about how the harmony, the guitar riffs, the drum beat, and the vocals all were working together to form this familiar sound and how those separate pieces of this musical puzzle all played a part in my long-forgotten memory. Of course, the artist who wrote this song has no idea that their creativity has triggered such a fond part of my past. I wonder what they would think if I told them?

What would *U* do if someone said that *U* left a lasting impression in their memory? Have *U* told someone they've left a positive mark in your life?

Something to **BREW** about.

# *Brew* U

No Applause, Please!

Since when did daytime television turn into one big thunderous applause?

I had the rare opportunity to watch some "talk" shows today, but there was more hand clapping than there was talking. Show after show – it seemed there was noise every 5 minutes!   I always thought applause was for something someone accomplished or a talent they demonstrated, not for adding cheese to a dish or a sweater to an outfit.

The more I watched (or rather listened) to the shows, the more aggravated I became.  Especially as I tried to read the lips of people who were talking. I couldn't believe how annoyed I was becoming and even more so because clapping is supposed to be a POSITIVE thing, and clearly I was viewing (listening) to it as negative.

This got me ***BREW***ing. Some people will clap when someone adds butter to bread, but how often do we cheer our friends or family on in life? Do *U* do so regularly? I know I need to do it more often. From here on out, I am going to make more of an effort to provide an encouraging word, acknowledge a positive move, give a pat on the back, and when necessary, I'll even offer up APPLAUSE.

# *Brew* **U**

Opposites Attract

Left or right? Which side do you think is your most attractive side?

An interesting study I read in Time found that people tend to favor their left side over their right. When I heard this on the news, several things came to mind:

1. Is my left side really better than my right? (Of course, I had to test that out in the mirror. I didn't notice a difference.)

2. Who came up with this study anyway?

3. We are always having to choose sides in life as it is. Now we are choosing to give one side of our body the upper hand over the other?

So, I decided rather than taking sides, I will take the opposite approach. It shouldn't be a certain facial profile that defines attractiveness. It shouldn't be physical attributes alone. It should be how we carry ourselves, our relation to others, and most of all, our relationship to ourselves. I realize that while I think I have some attractive attributes, there's always room for improvement.

Here's something to *BREW* over today.

Aside from the physical, what attracts *U* to certain people? More importantly, what do **U** find most attractive about *U*?

# *Brew* **U**

## Presence for the Holi-daze

*Warning: read with caution and a full heart.*

The holidays are here. Everywhere you look, there is music playing, commercials running, ornaments and shiny objects gleaming, but I've also noticed that not as many people are seeing the same thing: because their heads are buried in technology.

At first, I thought I was the only one who was noticing this, until a friend commented to me the other day about how long it took for the preparation, the meal, and the clean-up of their Thanksgiving: all because everyone was pausing to text, chat, etc. So, it's not just me.

Don't get me wrong: I enjoy all of the thrills that come with instant technology today. I think it is great to send a quick snapshot to family and friends who are away; look up a recipe real quickly, smartphone shop, even engage in Facebook, but I believe it is a matter of choosing when and where to use the technology. I am seeing and hearing about an increasing number of people who are too addicted to their gadgets: creating a sort of HOLI-DAZE; leaving the ones who are "with" them to fend for their own attention.

Ask me what my favorite holiday memories are and I'd have a laundry list of answers. As I settle into new territory this holiday season, I find myself ***BREW***ing over these memories now more than ever and I have discovered that the reason they are so near and dear to me is because everyone was present, in the Moment. No technology distractions. No Holi-Daze.

# *Brew* **U**

Remember a great aunt saying something outrageous? It is because you caught it in the moment (not hearing someone repeat what was just said because you missed it while you were "texting" someone else). Saw little Joey go crazy when he opened a gift? It is because you were watching him.

Will there not be any new memories made because of the craze of the Holi-Daze? I fear this upcoming generation will never realize how wonderful memories can be this time of year, or any time of year for that matter.

Have *U* noticed the same thing in your inner circles?

As we continue to shop and score deals on our gadgets (I am one of them!), I am definitely taking the time to give the best present I can: presence. Someday I hope it will be looked upon fondly, just as I fondly remember those who gave me the same gift: their presence.

*Brew* **U**

Say What?!?!

When was the last time you actually said to someone that you loved them?

A while back, our church issued a challenge to the married couples. In a series titled, "Honorable Homes," couples were asked to read Ephesians 5 and examine how being honorable to God first and foremost, can pave the way to becoming more honorable to each other which then creates a more "honorable home."

The couples were asked to answer a simple question: "What I wish my spouse would understand is _____." What would be your answer?

Answers varied between the men and women but there was one answer that stuck out for both sexes: each spouse wanted the other to understand that they loved them. But how often do they actually say it? As I ***BREW***ed over this, I realized this wasn't just a "marriage" thing. This could be applied to anyone in any relationship. A parent to a child. A brother to a sister. A friend to a friend.

Have *U* told someone special in your life that you love them? Do so now.
Now that *U* have told someone *U* love them, here are the answers given in the sessions above.

What Men Wanted Women to Understand:
 1. How much they actually do love them
 2. They need more encouragement/ intimacy

3. They're concerned about social media/distractions and desire more face to face time

4. They want their wives to engage in more financial communication

What Women Wanted Men to Understand:

1. They desire more emotional support & more "I love you"

2. They would like more face to face time – "date nights", hand-holding, and cuddling

3. They want their husbands to engage in healthy communication – less sports; more eye contact

4. They would like to see their husbands have a deeper walk with God

# *Brew* U

## Trash Talk

First, it was me. Now, it's my condo.

My place is undergoing what I call a "condo weight loss plan". I have been purging mass quantities of things to make a pending move a lot easier.

Today, it was my master bedroom closet that lost the most pounds. Hangers, duffel bags, suitcases, boxes, not a single area was untouched as I tossed away clothes that no longer fit, files and paperwork that no longer serve any purpose, and shoes that clearly should have been thrown away years ago!

As I tackled this project, I watched as my closet shelves began to get lighter. They became clear and open. Spacious. Ready for change. I ***BREW*** over how this exact experience was similar to my recent weight loss. As I cleared away the clutter that was my weight, and the circumstances that contributed to it, I began to get lighter. I became clear and open. Spacious. Ready for change.

Is there something within *U* that needs trashed? What is keeping *U* from tossing it away?

As I sit and look at the piles of trash bags by my front door, I know that with this "condo weight loss plan", I will gain more than I have ever imagined.

# *Brew* **U**

## Unleash the Hounds

During my morning workout at the gym, I watched as a woman passed by the window walking her dog on a leash. All of a sudden, the dog just stopped. Frozen in time. Staring straight ahead. The woman looked to see what the dog was looking at. It must not have been anything important because she gently started tugging on the leash to get the dog moving again. The dog stood still. She then tugged a little harder, (still somewhat gentle) to persuade her pet to take a step. Still nothing.

She stood there for a few minutes watching the dog. The dog in turn, watched whatever was ahead and was insistent on staying put. Finally, after several minutes, she tugged the leash a bit harder, the dog's neck outstretched slightly, but stood still. The woman then reached behind and gently nudged the dog on the backside and the dog started walking again.

As I watched this scene unfold, I couldn't help but ***BREW*** over how sometimes I can be just like the dog. Not willing to move. Staying put. Frozen in time. Fear of moving forward. Too cautious. Just plain stubborn. God is just like the dog owner - gently nudging me, trying to get me to move while being patient until finally, I need a gentle swat to get going.

I realize that God is not going to steer me in the wrong direction, much like the woman walking her dog. The leash is there to guide, protect, and shelter. I need to be more cognizant of that and realize that when God is tugging at

Brew **U**

my leash it's for a good reason. I need to unleash the fears within.

What about *U*?  Does your leash need tugged?

PS: To the dog lovers out there, this woman was not in any way hurting her dog. I promise. No hate mail, please.

# *Brew* U

## What Does Your Welcome Mat Say?

Have you ever walked into a place and thought, "I totally feel at home here"? (Your current home does not count.)

I experienced that on a recent shopping trip. The Moment I walked into a "Charming Charlie" store, my first reaction was: this place was made for me!!

But it wasn't the jewelry and accessories at this boutique that caught my eye at first (although they were great). It was the environment. It was like stepping foot inside a huge crayon box and making your way through the rows and shades of colors. There was the blue section. Reds had their own spot. Gold and silver staked claim in another area. Prints, pastels, and other unique finds each had their own special place.  The clear and shiny floors along with the mirrors dispersed around the store gave it a clean and inviting look. The second thing that caught my attention was the customer service. The girls working that day were friendly, attentive, and knowledgeable. In fact, their bright personalities matched the decor!

I felt completely at home in this place as though a special welcome mat was set outside the door with my name on it. This got me *BREW*ing over how welcome I make people feel. Whether they are life-long friends, family members, or complete strangers, do people feel like they are at home in my presence?  Do they feel valued and appreciated? What does my welcome mat say?

How about *U*? What does your welcome mat say?

# *Brew* **U**

## Your Field of Vision

As I write this, I am recovering from retina re-attachment surgery. I am now 4 weeks without vision in one eye and it has been, pardon the pun, very eye-opening.

Immediately following my surgery, I had to spend days with my head upright for 30 minutes followed with my head face down for the remaining 30 minutes. Every hour it was the same. This went on for quite a few days. I would rest my forehead on my elbows, on a table, lie on my bed, or on the ground face down. While annoying, it gave me a lot of time to actually think about the "vision" for my life going forward.

I guess you could equate it to meditating. With limited TV and computer use because I couldn't see, combined with lying face down for half of my waking hours, I was able to *BREW* quite a bit. I would analyze and think about where I have been, where I am going, what I would like to change and how to handle those things that I cannot change. I also thought of goals, dreams, aspirations, and ways to tackle upcoming stresses once my vision fully returns.

What situations have forced *U* to look inside yourself? Did *U* find that you were lying face down, avoiding the true vision for *U*? Do *U* now see yourself in a different light?

*Brew* **U**

Appreciation Nation

Yes, life is full of ups and downs. Yes, there are always bumps in the road. Yes, life is a journey not a destination.

But I would have never imagined that my journey over the past few months would be riddled with potholes, smooth patches, and then complete drop-offs.

Over the course of several weeks I have gotten married, grieved the unexpected death of my Mother, received a raise, and am now preparing myself for a major move (with a possible career change to boot!) Needless to say: my physical, mental, and emotional self has been tied and untied in knots.

In the midst of all of this and through a lot of spiritual guidance, I have been ***BREW***ing over the word "appreciate" and have become reacquainted with the definition and the importance it plays in my life. As I witness marriages falling apart, I appreciate the one that I do have. While she is gone physically, I find that I appreciate my Mother now more than ever before. I appreciate the support I have received from my family and my friends in the recent celebrations and the heartbreaking moments of late. I appreciate the fact that I currently have a job. I appreciate the opportunities that lie ahead.

Appreciation has actually been my physical, mental, and emotional healing. I believe if the entire country could adopt an "Appreciation Nation" attitude, we'd all be better for it. I know that I will continue to look to appreciation as my guide in ways that I hope will mold my future.

What do *U* appreciate? In what ways can *U* use appreciation more effectively?

# *Brew* **U**

How Did You Get to Where You Are Going

When was the last time you thought, "How did I end up here?"

Today? Yesterday? Last month? Last year?

I recently did some freelance work for TheRealSkinny.net and the site's founder, Mary Fox. It's been highly rewarding, not just on a personal level, but also on a professional level. And as a result, I ventured into different realms of the media world.

Isn't it amazing how we never know where we are going to end up? Certain days can seem like carbon copies of the days before yet when we look back over a specific amount of time, there is always change. Sometimes the changes are subtle. Sometimes the changes are monumental. Sometimes they are bad and sometimes they are good. But there's always change.

Knowing this has got me ***BREW***ing: not as much about the past or the present, but rather the future.

Where will I end up next?

Where do *U* hope to end up next?

# *Brew* U

## Is Your (Blank) Clean?

There's something about cleanliness that drives me to think differently and do strange things.

A clean car leads me to believe it's running better.
A clean refrigerator persuades me to make better food choices.
A clean bedroom helps me sleep better at night (or so I think).
A clean closet simply makes me feel calmer.

I am ***BREW***ing over this after a recent bout of frustration which sent me on a cleaning spree. I instantly felt better after I did it. It is as though my scrubbing, wiping, mopping, and dusting were subconsciously cleaning out my internal mind and clearing my own clutter within.

How do *U* clear your internal clutter? What do *U* strive to always keep clean?

# *Brew* **U**

Lesson Plans

This week, my neighbor took me to lunch.

At 85 years young, there is not a single topic that is off limits. She's shared so much with me about her life: her childhood, her marriage, her kids, her career as a managing editor, and everything in between. Having grown up just outside of New York City, she has witnessed a lot of change and as I write this, she continues to deal with change as a retiree in Southwest Florida.

Over the past three years, she's been what they call, "neighborly." Nurturing, friendly, welcoming, but most of all, she's been a great teacher. I have learned a lot from our conversations such as how each round of change brings opportunities to grow and excel.

After our lunch, I began to ***BREW*** over the changes I have experienced so far in life and what I've learned from them. Here are just a few:

Change:  moving to Florida from Ohio fresh out of college and not knowing a soul in my new surroundings.
Lesson Learned: Self-growth, self-awareness, independence, and true friendship.

Change: lightning fast, life-changing technology.
Lesson Learned:  Today's technology is a luxury, but real relationships are first and foremost

## *Brew* **U**

Change: uprooting my Florida lifestyle and replacing my sandals, tank tops and "single" status for boots, sweaters, and a new family in Maine.
Lesson Learned: With love, all things are possible.

What changes have *U* witnessed in your life that have impacted *U* most? What lesson did *U* learn from it?

# *Brew* U

Wood Slippers for the Princess

It may be called "Princess", but this is no fairy tale. I am referring to a show I watched on CNBC.

"Princess" is a competitive-reality show that teaches 20-something women the value of money. In each half hour episode, a "Princess" is featured showcasing how she is foolishly spending her money, using others to get by financially, and demonstrates no signs of improving her situation responsibly.

In walks Gail Vaz-Oxlade, the hard-nosed financial expert, who drills the girls about their current spending habits. She strips them of their financial so-called freedom in an effort to teach them the way the world and money really work. I equate it to taking away their glass slippers and replacing them with wood ones. Through a series of exercises, they learn the importance of saving and the best ways to spend. It's a hard lesson for them to learn but in the end, if they do well, they do win some money to pay down their debt or to pay back those people they've used in the past for monetary gain.

I wish this show was around when I was younger. As I sit and watch, I **BREW** over my own financial blunders – many of them in my early to late 20's. I had my fair share of wood slippers during those days. Do *U* recall your days of wood slippers? (Or for the men who are reading this, your wood shoes?)

# *Brew* U

I highly recommend any late teen and early 20-somethings watch this.

I would go as far as to recommend parents DVR it for their kids. Schools, too. It can conjure up a lot of discussion in the classroom. It's a valuable tool.

# *Brew* **U**

## Personal Sound Effects

Recently, I caught a mini-marathon of Sound FX on NFL Network. And I must admit, my cheeks hurt from smiling and laughing after watching numerous episodes. I absolutely love watching and most of all, listening, to the players and coaches in their environment: their frustrations, their happiness, their endurance, and most of all their funny and random quotes.

I adore words. And I love to listen to people. In fact, when I was on a trip through Europe, I kept a list of random quotes and sentences I heard people say.

That random quote idea came to life again when I was working in a TV newsroom. The random things people would say, how they would say it, where they would say it, and other people's perceptions of it really made for some comic relief during some tense working Moments.

I ***BREW*** over this while thinking about what it would be like if I were to mic'd up during various stages of my life and turned into my own Sound FX episode. How would I come across? How did I handle happy, sad, and silly situations? What would the listener think?

Would *U* ever want to be mic'd up? How do *U* think others would react to your sound effects? How do *U* think *U* would perceive yourself?

# *Brew* U

### I'll take 'My Life' for $1000, Alex

If your life were a category on the Jeopardy game board, what would the answers (or should I say questions) be?

What would *U* want people to know about you? What areas of your life would you *U* not want to see on the big electronic quiz screen?

Now that I've got you ***BREW***ing about this, imagine that your closest friends and family were the contestants. What would they get right? What would they get wrong? What if one of those not-so-great areas of your life did make the big board. How would they react? Would they still be your friends?

Similar to a game show, our lives can really put us to the test. I've discovered over the years that I need to act as if Alex Trebek is following me around and taking notes, strategizing with producers as to what my game pieces will entail. With this said, I have learned that no matter what my situation, treat people with respect. Do what is right as best as I know how. Always be sure that those who matter to me know it. Be true to myself, always. This way, I will not be fearful over what will make the board and what won't.

*Brew* **U**

Where's Your Recliner?

It's no secret – we humans love our comfort zones. I compare them to recliners.

As a little girl, I remember my father had a certain seat and row he liked to sit in at church. This worked to my advantage knowing exactly where to find my parents, or hide from them, if I wanted to.

At home, we each had our unspoken "recliners" at mealtime. No one had to tell you where to sit. You just knew. In school, we had assigned seats. From what I remember, it was usually alphabetically. I fondly remember locating my desk and making it my own for the year, stacking the shelf with my folders, pencils, pens, etc.

And into adulthood, it continues. We are assigned seats on airplanes. (And we often pray the person that will be assigned next to us is bearable!). Ever notice the looks on people's faces as they search for their seat? Hesitantly, they walk down the aisle. Then when they find it, you see an instant sigh come across their face. It's their seat. Their assigned spot. Their recliner for the moment.

I am **BREW**ing about this, because recently at a high school basketball game, I saw someone's "recliner" fall victim to another. The look of confusion, disgust, and agitation was clearly evident. I am confident that for the rest of the night, they felt out of their comfort zone. Their "recliner" had been hijacked!

# *Brew* U

We love our recliners: a place that's cozy, comfortable, and just feels friendly and familiar.

What about *U*? Where is your recliner? What makes your recliner so special?

# *Brew* **U**

## People Skills

I read an interesting passage this week: "A person can change your life. A person can change your day. People are everything."

I immediately began to *BREW*. "A person change your life." I thought about some of the people who have changed mine. Sure, family members. But a large percentage of my "life changers" were people I would have never suspected to handle such a feat! They are people I would meet randomly out in public, at businesses, or in a social setting. In most instances, I didn't even know they were changing my life until after the change happened.

"A person can change your day." Isn't that the truth? The employer who offers you the job. The doctor that calls with news. The driver that cuts you off in traffic. Or the person that brings you flowers at the end of a day.

"People are everything." Without people, there would be nothing. Given our technological lifestyle these days, I think sometimes we forget that the person looking at our Facebook status updates, texts, and Instagram pictures, is indeed, a "person." They have emotions, feelings, thoughts, everything that digital lacks.

What about *U*: who has changed your life? Who has changed your day?

*Brew* **U**

## Decisions, Decisions

Here's a quick personal survey. When it comes to making decisions, you:
1) make decisions quickly; whether or not they are correct.
2) take a bit of time to make a decision
3) wait until the very last minute to make a decision

I can honestly say I am all of the above. I ***BREW*** about this because recently I had a day where I had to make more than my usual fair share of decisions and it was exhausting! Then, just a few days later, I found myself reading a book with an entire chapter devoted to making decisions! In that moment, I made a decision that I would finish that chapter later.  Gee!  I just made another decision!

At times, I find myself thinking back to the wrong decisions I made. (Which in itself can be a bad decision!) But in my mind, I try to navigate my way around my course of thinking at that time: why did I make that decision? What were the factors that led up to the decision? I decide I am going to make decisions differently.

I once read where choosing not to make a decision was actually a decision in itself. Is your head spinning? Mine is. Take a look back at some of your decisions: which ones were good? Which were bad? How do *U* handle decisions now as opposed to before?

Free Maintenance

Today I am ***BREW***ing over the word "resolution".

We hear this word a thousand times as the New Year approaches. When U hear the word resolution, what comes to mind? Diet? Exercise? Debt Management? Motivation? Failure? Challenge? Waste of Time? Annoying?

Instead of "resolution", I have decided to replace this overused word with "maintenance." Here's why:

1.  Often times, people can shell out lots of money towards whatever it is they are "resolving" to do. (For example, additional diet aids, fancy new exercise equipment - for those who have weight "resolutions") My "maintenance plan" costs nothing!

2.  The word "resolution" can sound intimidating to some. Maintenance is simply maintaining. No far reaching aspirations that seem out of reach. No frustrations. No mixed emotions. Maintaining seems simpler to me.

So, what is on my maintenance plan?

1.  My physical health. Over the past few years, I have learned to listen to my body so I know my limits, challenges, and obstacles that can help or hinder my physical maintenance plan. (I should add here that my physical health maintenance plan consists of things I can control; I realize not every physical ailment that develops is controllable by me.)

# *Brew* U

2.  My emotional health. I am so thankful for my family, friends, and colleagues. I will continue to maintain my strong friendships and professional relationships. How easy and cost effective is that?

3.  My spiritual health. I find that by maintaining my spiritual self, I actually end up gaining. Free Spiritual Maintenance is always guaranteed!

What about *U*? What would *U* put on your free maintenance plan?

# *Brew* **U**

## Tap Your APP

How many apps do you have on your smartphone? How many new apps have you downloaded since receiving that phone?

As the saying goes, there truly is an app for that! There's an app for finding the best gas prices. Restaurants have apps. Stores have apps. Everything that you can possibly think of has an app. There's even an app you can download for amusing reading while using the restroom!

This app thing got me to ***BREW***ing. People love apps so why aren't humans like apps? Let me explain:

Apps are designed to be ready when you are. You touch. It performs.  Are you ready at a Moment's notice to help someone in need? They also are also designed to give us answers to prices, deals, services, etc. Are you giving your best when it comes to family, friends, work, and other ventures?

App creators put a lot of thought and time into making sure apps are pleasing to the eye and easy to navigate. Are you welcoming to people? Do *U* take the time to present yourself in the most admirable light? Do *U* take much thought in how you interact with others?

What if there was an app specifically designed about *U*? What would it look like? What service would *U* provide?

# *Brew* U

## Ants Marching

It's 6:45 am.

I've just been through an intense workout.

As I returned home from the gym, the only thing on my mind is breakfast and a nice cup of coffee.

So you can imagine my surprise when I get home to find that ants have invaded my coffee maker. They were everywhere. On the buttons. In the water filter. Under the coffee maker. On top of the coffee maker. They were hanging out near the electrical cord that leads to the coffee maker. Everywhere. And boy, did the sight really send shivers up my spine.

 I cleaned up what I could and did a little internet investigating. The information superhighway was filled with ideas, tricks, suggestions, and remedies to this problem. With time ticking, and a job to report to, all I could do was take note and resolve to fix it later. But of course, I was without my morning coffee. As I got ready for work, I quickly realized how lost I was without my morning ritual.

This has me ***BREW***ing. Isn't it amazing how quickly we gravitate to habits? How lost we become when our schedule or ritual is changed?

How do *U* cope?

*Brew* **U**

## You Take the Cake

I adore cake. I look forward to birthdays, weddings, showers, for the simple fact that there's a strong possibility there will be cake.

While I enjoy many types of cake – my personal favorite is white cake with white icing. Very plain Jane in the world that we live in today which consists of creative, unique, and specialty flavored cakes and cupcakes. I am ***BREW***ing over this after receiving this month's Food Network Magazine and saw that they have a cake for every month! (Imagine my delight!!)

January – Ultimate Vanilla Cake
February – Chocolate Blackout Cake
March – Grasshopper Cake
April – Lemon Meringue Cake
May – Cookies and Cream Cake
June – Berry Ice Cream Cake
July – Pina Colada Cake
August – S'mores Cake
September – Honey Apple Almond Cake
October – Chocolate-Orange Cake with Salted Caramel
November – Maple Walnut Cake
December – Black and White Mocha Cake

How about *U*? Does your birthday cake match your personality? Or better yet, if *U* were to be a cake, what flavor would *U* be?

# *Brew* **U**

### Is That How I Look When I Drive?

"Is that how I look when I drive?"

That's what my husband asked while we were on a trip. No, it wasn't the driver he was eluding to, it was the vehicle. This car looked exactly like his new one. I could sense the pride he felt in looking at his same car and how it glided on the pavement, shimmered in the sun, while projecting a quiet, yet sporty attitude.

It was funny at first to watch him look at the car we passed. But then it got me to **BREW**ing. If I were to examine myself outside of my own body, what would I see?

Would I see someone who is kind to others? Would I see a warm disposition? Do I look calm, cool, and collected? Do I look frazzled? Annoyed? Angry?

What do *U* think people see when they look at *U*? Better yet, what do *U* imagine *U* look like?

*Brew* **U**

## Social Media Musings

No, this is not about how internet surfing can lead to sedentary lifestyles and consequential weight gain (although true in some instances). Instead, I am focusing on how social media could be expanding waistlines in a different way: through the constant postings of recipes!

If I gained a pound for every time I saw someone post a recipe, forward a recipe, pin a recipe, or tweet a dish or product, I would weigh 100,000 pounds! And a million dollars in debt just to purchase the ingredients for said recipes.

But, as I ***BREW*** about this, I find I am not completely innocent. A few dishes spotted online have provoked me to give them a whirl, but not every single one I see. Personally, this constant parade of recipe sharing is actually turning me off. To the point where I am considering ignoring a few of the people I follow just so my eyes (and stomach) can get some peace and quiet!

Now to *U*. Maybe it's not recipes per say, but is there something on social media that is aggravating *U*? What have *U* done about it?

# *Brew* U

## (not good) GREAT Sports-Men-Ship

As I write this, sports fans are embarking on what many would call the epicenter of the year. It is October. With multiple sports franchises and leagues in action, this is the time of year when remotes get really active and schedules start to get more intense.

While football is my favorite sport, I do enjoy watching other sports. But most of all, I love hearing the banter among my guy friends who choose to debate, philosophize, analyze, and even pick on each other over plays, teams, strategies, and anything else that is sport-related.

Every once in a while I will offer my two cents and sometimes my comments are well received! Better yet, sometimes I will get a text, a call, or an email in regard to an observation over something sports related from my inner circle of guy friends. I actually find that almost humbling in that they will pause to think about me, the girl, in that Moment. I ***BREW*** over this because I learned this week just how blessed I was to have the close guy friends that I have.

Do ***U*** have great sports-men-ships? How have they impacted your life?

*Brew* **U**

Back to the Food-ture

Isn't it amazing how food can take you back in time?
The sight. The smell. Even the sound of certain foods can
trigger memories.

Over the past year, I've been exposed to different foods and
traditions that my husband and his family enjoy. He's also
learned (and tasted) some of my family's specialties and
has learned what makes our family tick in the food
department. What really has me ***BREW***ing is that with
each edible item, there's a story or fond recollection.

For example, my Mom makes outstanding buckeyes. What
makes our family smile is not only the chocolate and
peanut butter goodness, but how they are always stored in
this certain container. Once we spot the "buckeye" bowl,
we know life is about to get a little sweeter.

Below, I've listed a few "Back to the Food-ture (Future)"
items that are hot on my memory list and why.

1. Mom's Buckeye's (and Container as mentioned above)
and her twice baked potatoes.
2. "Dad's Breakfast": a special breakfast Dad always
makes. It's even more special now that I live so far away.
3. Stadium Mustard: it always triggers the senses associated
with going to sporting events with the family in Cleveland.
4. Aunt Margaret's Christmas Cookies: fond memories of
making these with Mom over the holidays with the Ohio
snowfall outside

*Brew* **U**

5. Covered Bridge Pizza: countless memories of this popular local pizza joint with friends and family

And I trust there's more traditions ***BREW***ing in the food-ture now that I am newly married.

What about *U*? What are your back to the food-tures?

# *Brew* **U**

## Cabanas and Condos

Currently, I'm on vacation in North Carolina. My husband and I have been surveying various areas in a quest to determine where we will live once we leave Maine.

Among the "hot spots" are condos along Carolina Beach. There's also neighborhoods on the outskirts of the beach which provide more of the family suburbs type of environment.

As we looked at each living environment, I began to *BREW* over the pros and cons of each.

Could I live here every day? Where would I work? Would the surroundings drive me crazy after a while or would they always be enjoyable? In the midst of all of this, there's also my husband's feelings to consider. What are his pros? His cons? How do they differ from mine? How will we compromise?

The final decision and the final destination will make the journey an interesting one.

But in the end, the best decision will be the one where we are together.

What about *U*? Are *U* living in your dream destination? What makes it right for *U*?

# *Brew* **U**

## File It Away

On game day, most football fans surround themselves with snacks, drinks, and well, other fans. I've surrounded myself with a pile of documents and a paper shredder.

Call it the Saturday "fall cleaning" of my file boxes. With each commercial break, the sounds of the college football game are replaced with the humming sound of the shredder: document after document evaluated, sorted, and prepared to face their final destiny as tiny scraps.

If only our problems could be this easy. As I shred, I **BREW**: wouldn't it be nice if we could just take whatever is bugging us and send it through a machine, never to be seen again? But that's not reality. I can only do what I can here on earth and file the rest away to God. He will do the shredding in His time.

What are some problems *U* would love to see shredded? Have *U* dealt with them as best *U* can? And most importantly, have *U* filed the rest away in the appropriate place with shredding to take place later?

# *Brew* U

## Grad-U-ation

"What are <u>you</u> going to do next?"  "Where do <u>you</u> go from here?"  "What are <u>your</u> plans for the future?"

Graduates are bombarded with these questions and a whole lot more during graduation season.  Notice how all of the questions pertain to the word '<u>you</u>'? It's only fitting that in the middle of the word graduation is "**U**"!

In this day of social media, graduates already know what it's like to live in the world of "**U**". Many don't even blink an eye when it comes to posting personal information, opinions, thoughts, annoyances or otherwise. Some can't even tether themselves away from their devices for a single Moment to even notice what is going on around them.  I can't help but wonder how this will help or hinder their lives ahead. Will they continue to be consumed in the world of "**U**" or will they attend the "U of Life" by simply taking the plunge and submersing themselves in the world around them and absorb all life has to offer?

For graduates, and those around them, the focus now moves from the life they've known to a future life in the unknown. A place where I believe a sense of community and belonging will be of the most importance; this is what I like to call the "U of Life".

 As I ***BREW*** about this, I can't help but be reminded of the people that helped and advised me during those first few years in the unknown. It was their advice, character,  and the way they role modeled their professional and personal lives that really had the most impact on me in the early classes of the "U of Life" – and I still use what I have learned today.

What do *U* remember about your graduation years? Who has influenced *U* in the U of Life? Who continues to do so?

*Brew* **U**

## Hairs the Situation

Is there someone in your life that you simply can't fathom living without? If so, who? And why?

I'm going to ask this question again. If your first answer was your spouse/significant other, your kids, your parents, or even God: eliminate them from your choices.

Now, is there someone in your life that you simply can't fathom living without? If so, who? And why?

For me, my hairdresser is one. I'm **BREW**ing over this because today is just one of a few visits I remain with her before I move out of state.

Like most women (and maybe some men), Tammy is more than just a hairdresser.

1)    She was one of the first real friends I made when I moved to Florida nearly 15 years ago.

2)    She has always had my best interest at heart, both professionally and personally.

3)    She's been a great therapist!

4)    She's outstanding at her craft.

5)    She's put up with me as I change hairstyles constantly: from short to long, long to short, – and has

always given me her honest opinion especially as I've changed physically.

She's fantastic and it will be hard to not have her around when I move. I appreciate her more than words can say, but I am going to let her know as much as possible in the coming weeks that remain with her.

Back to that question I asked you earlier: have *U* told this person how much *U* appreciate what they have done in your life?

## I'm a Loser

Tonight, I will watch one of my favorite finales on television – The Biggest Loser.

This is the big "reveal" episode where all of the participants will show off their new selves after their individual weight loss. As with every season finale to date, there will be some new clothes, new hair colors, and especially new renowned confidence in themselves.

Having lost more than 150 pounds myself, I too, am a Loser. However, I did not have a trainer. I did not have a ranch. I did not have workout partners – I pretty much did everything on my own. I was my ranch. I was my trainer. I was my own workout partner.

I did not have a big reveal. I did not have a glaring spotlight showing off my accomplishments. I was not interviewed about my success. But I did not want any of those things. Here's what I DID have:

1. Friends and family who supported me continually throughout the process.

2. My own personal trainer: me. I knew I would have to work to achieve what I wanted. It is  amazing what you discover about yourself in solitude: your beliefs, values, worth all come to the surface when focused on you.

3. God. He is the one that the Loser spotlight should be focused on. He is the one who gave me the strength,

courage, security, and the drive to continue to transform myself.

As I sit and watch tonight's Losers, I will also **BREW** over my own personal achievement. While there are more "accomplishments" to be had, I am thankful that I was able to gain loser status on the scale.

What has been your biggest achievement? What do *U* still have left to accomplish. What will be your Loser Moment?

# *Brew* U

Let's Play the Waiting Game

Take a moment and think about your closest friends and family.

Chances are, there's someone within your circle that is going through a situation that's mentally, physically, or emotionally taxing. Perhaps it's financial hardship. A health concern. A family struggle. A loss. A gain. Whatever it may be, often times it's a situation that only we can control for so long. Then it's up to God to do the rest.

For those who are spiritually inclined, this is where prayer, patience, and faith set in. I am dealing with something right now that involves an incredible amount of prayer, patience, and faith. While this in itself can be difficult for some, I find the hardest part is waiting. I am a chronic planner. If I can't "do" something about it, then I do what I falsely consider the next best thing: thinking.

Thinking turns into processing. Then I ***BREW*** things over in my mind. More thinking. More processing. More ***BREW***ing. But no matter how fast I spin those mental wheels, I am not going anywhere.

I need to learn to wait. So as I wait, wait, and wait some more, I am curious to know what *U* do when *U* have time to wait? How do *U* handle it? How do *U* play the waiting game?

*Brew* **U**

Physical Attributes

I have a whole new appreciation for those who devote their lives to our physical health and well-being.

I have worked as a journalist in the healthcare industry and I've learned a lot about the physical body. I've witnessed various surgeries, delicate situations, and how those in the profession have to balance the educational and emotional side of this care. There are several people in my life that I admire and ***BREW*** about often.

1. My Mother, the Pharmacist. While I have witnessed her educate people and provide medical assistance, she is incredibly smart and constantly educating herself and bettering herself in her field for the benefit of patients everywhere.

2. My husband, the Kidney Dialysis Technician. He works in an extremely delicate environment, thinks fast on his feet, while providing compassionate care to those whose lives are literally in his hands!

3. My primary care physician. She doesn't beat around the bush. She'll be frank with you. I love that.

What about *U*? Is there a profession that *U* admire – and why?

# *Brew* **U**

## Interior Decorating

When I was a little girl, I would closely examine the fronts of houses. Based on how the windows were spaced and where the front door was placed, I would picture each house with a "face". (I know, I am strange.)

Some houses look happy. Some look sad. Some puzzled and some even look shy!

As I would observe each house, I would often wonder, "What is going on in there?"

I began **BREW**ing over this memory for many reasons.

After recently watching a show about houses on TV, contestants (home owners) are asked to visit each other's homes and judge the interior and exterior based on various criteria. I was amazed at how each contestant would take the interior criticism personally as if it was reflection of their own interior selves! I got to looking at my own place, wondering what people would say about it. Would I be offended at a negative remark about my place? Could I brush it off? Could *U* if it was about your home's interior?

There are also people in my life who are establishing "new homes." What will their new interior look like? Will their decorating be a reflection of themselves? Take a look at your surroundings – are they a reflection of *U*?

As a 5 year old, I would question the home's interior based on its exterior "face." As a 38 year old, I examine the interior hearts of that dwelling. And isn't that real interior decorating? It doesn't matter what stuff you have or don't have, where it's placed, how much, or how little you own.

As long as it's decorated in love, compassion, integrity, trust, and respect, you're fully furnished!

# *Brew* U

Seasons Feelings

During a recent outing in the blustery winter weather of Maine, my husband looked over at me and said, "I can't wait until we move out of this state." I agree.

I know many people who reach a point in the woes of winter where things are very bleak. The lack of sunshine, the blowing winds, and bitter cold temperatures can begin to take their toll. For some, I know depression, despair, and impatience begin to set in which makes the remaining winter season almost unbearable.

I began to **BREW**. Can the same thing be said for the different seasons we face in our lives? When seasons in life are good, we tend to feel upbeat similar to a bright, shiny and comfortable day. When seasons are not so great, frustration, anxiety, depression, and sadness can creep in. Interestingly, I am dealing with my first winter in more than a decade and at the same time, I am faced with a trying "season" in my life. Talk about seasons feelings!

We still have some time until we move, so we have to make the best of the current season that we are in. While everyone has their own individual way, I do know that one thing we will continue to do is count our blessings, regardless of the season or the feeling we endure.

How do *U* handle the changing seasons and feelings in your life? When you look back on the difficult seasons, is there anything *U* would have done differently?

# *Brew* U

## Tiny Tunes

Ever notice how much music now plays a part in our everyday life? I'm not just talking about hearing it on the radio or singing it in church.

Take sports for instance. Music isn't just used for the introduction of the game or in and out of commercials breaks. Now, every time a graphic is shown, the music fades in. I call these tiny tunes. At first, I was annoyed by it. Now, it seems natural. These tiny tunes have me *BREW*ing. Imagine if we saw something on the screen and it was silent?

At baseball games: batters now use tiny tunes to walk up to the plate. I know it's used to jazz up the crowd and pump up the player, but do you remember when batters used to walk up to just applause? When were these tiny tunes decided?

Even when we power up our digital devices these tiny tunes produce a jingle. What would happen if we powered up in silence?

Even commercials are leaving out words and driving their message with music.

Don't get me wrong. I love music. I love all kinds of music and I don't necessarily hate any of these things I have mentioned, I just have taken a huge notice to these tiny tunes.

# *Brew* U

Are there things changing in your life that have strangely captured your attention? It doesn't have to be music necessarily, but maybe it's something that *U* are noticing more and more? What are the "tiny tunes" in your life?

# *Brew* **U**

## We Value Your Opinion

On a recent outing to Chick-Fil-A, I was asked to fill out a comment card.

I was happy to do so because I love this particular location/staff, and the food! There was no agenda to do so. No coupon. No frills. Nothing. They asked. I did it. Often times, people fill out comment cards because they have something to complain about – not the opposite. But as most of you know, I am not one to shy away from telling someone (or business) how much I enjoy their service.

I had to rate the following: professionalism, attitude, attentiveness, efficiency, environment, and overall experience.

This got me **BREW**ing over my own life. What if I were the focus of a comment card? How would my friends and colleagues rate the above? What about my past and present employers?
What areas need improvement? Which areas rate best?

How would people rate *U*? What areas of the comment card do *U* need to work on?

# *Brew* **U**

## You Da Man

Sure, he hollered at me when I talked back.

Yes, he grounded me when my report card wasn't the best.

And he definitely made me do chores I didn't want to do.

But, that's what made my Dad a great Father. As a teenager, I certainly brought my fair share of tension and rebellion to our relationship, but despite our tense Moments, my Dad still was loving and supportive, yet firm.

Hardworking and strong in faith, my Dad taught me the power of self: How to be independent. How to be kind to others. How to be hard-working. How to be a friend. How to be good, upstanding, and moral. And most of all: how to love.

*BREW*ing over what I have learned from my Dad,  I believe it's important to recognize ALL of the men in our lives who have helped to shape us into who we are today, biological or not.

Who are the men in your life that have helped shape *U*? What did *U* learn from them? Do they know what kind of impact they had on *U*?

# *Brew* **U**

## Have You Laughed Today?

Have you laughed today?

Every Christmas season, I think of comedian, Jim Gaffigan. During a stand-up special a few years ago, he commented on how "strange" our holiday traditions are.

1. We go outside, chop down a tree, drag it into the living room and proceed to "decorate it for Jesus."

2. We take our lights from inside the house and string them outside.

3. We choose to hang our socks over the fire and fill them with candy.

So, from time to time, I'll look at my decorations and laugh. Today was one of them. I'm *BREW*ing over this because over the past several days, I have not seen too many people laughing. They are too busy engaged in the hectic holiday season. You can see the earthly tensions on their faces when really it should be the spiritual joy, peace, and comfort that we should be engaged in.

What about *U*? Do *U* get caught up in the "holiday hectic" season? Is there a way *U* can replace that tension with laughter?

*Brew* **U**

## Find Your Lane

I recently saw a car commercial that was quick to highlight the new design, the technologically advanced interior and the attention to detail that the manufacturer put into the driver and the car's overall performance. At the end of the commercial, the ad stated, "Find Your Own Lane."

And I began to ***BREW:*** "Find Your Own Lane." This could be applied to life. We are bombarded with so many questions, choices, decisions, demands and at times, we may be tempted to stray into another lane in order to meet the needs, criteria, or acceptance of others. My mind was racing: have I strayed into another lane? Have I found my own lane? Am I staying within my own lane? What exactly is my lane? Where does my lane lead? What exactly does my lane consist of?

How about *U?* Have *U* picked your lane? Do *U* tend to wander into another lane? Where does your lane lead?

# *Brew* **U**

### Your New Year Starts Today

"A year from now you will have wished you started today."
I read that quote recently and it has been ***BREW***ing within
me ever since.

You can apply that phrase to so many things: weight loss,
financial situations, mending relationships, work, etc.

I remember hitting that 1 year mark when I first started my
weight loss journey. I was so thankful to have been able to
accomplish as much as I had even though I knew I had a
long way to go. It was a huge sigh of relief to know I was
in a different place than I was a year ago.

That said, there are other situations where I need to kick my
butt into gear and apply that quote today. A year from now
I will be glad I did.

What about *U*? Your New Year starts today: what do *U* set
out to accomplish?

*Brew* **U**

## Womanly Shape

Mom. Many of us will take the time to honor her on Mother's Day. She undoubtedly deserves some pampering and appreciation for her guidance, sacrifice, and love.

But I am ***BREW***ing today over a challenge to go one step further. Honor all of the women who have had a positive influence on your life and do so throughout the year. I have quite a few women in my life who have shaped me into who I am today and for that, I am thankful.

Not everyone may have someone they call "Mom." Some may have lost their Mom physically, mentally or otherwise.

Some women may never be called "Mom", yet provide the same advice, support, and unconditional love that a Mom would.

Think back on the women who have helped shape your life in a positive way. Perhaps a call or email is in order?

Are *U* up to challenge?

# *Brew* U

## The ABzzzz's of Camping

There's nothing like your own bed after you've been camping.

While I don't mind the outdoors, the constant exposure to creature comforts such as air conditioning and comfy mattresses makes outside living a challenge to me.

During two steamy nights along the North Carolina coastline, I listened to an array of sounds from my tent: crickets, rustling branches and leaves, and other various critters. But along with nature's evening chorus came thunderous-like clapping from humans: in the form of snoring. (Those at fault will remain nameless)

As I listened to what I called the "Snoring Symphony" (because it was not just one person). At one point I said to someone on the trip, "I don't even hear the critters anymore. Did they bail?" A small giggle after that statement was quickly drowned out by the snoring symphony.

I began to **BREW** over how I thought camping was fun back in the day and now that I am older, it's lost its appeal. I had a good time on this trip. The company was absolutely fabulous but the lack of restful sleep due to the evening snoring concert (and the heat) really took its toll.

Are there things that *U* loved to do once and now *U* don't?

# *Brew* **U**

### Your there! You're their!

How many of you smirked at the above title?

Did you correct the title of this title in your mind?

Did you even notice anything about the title?

Before you roll your eyes, no, this is not a lesson on proper grammar. I am ***BREW***ing over this because of a recent Moment I had with my husband's teenage son.

Over the past few weeks, he and I have shared funny Facebook postings, TV segments, signs, and anything that has to do with grammar and the misuse of it. During a trip to Boston last month, he actually sought me out to show me a store sign that was blatantly using the word "are" when it should have said "our."

It warms my heart to know that he associates me with grammar. Something useful. I find that being a role-model for something that will remain a positive in someone's life can sometimes be the best compliment.

Who do *U* look to when it comes to important things in life? Who has influenced *U* in a positive way?

# *Brew* U

## What's Your Logo?

Monopoly. Chutes & Ladders. Hungry, Hungry Hippos. Twister. Remember those games? They were simple. Not much to them.

Fast forward to the games of today. I saw a board game in a store recently called "The Logo Game." Talk about marketing at its best! Designed like Monopoly, the box was covered in logos and on the back were some of the game's sample cards. One had four different Mexican food items and the player had to guess the logo or business. (In this case, it was Taco Bell.) There was also a brown package (this was UPS).

This type of game makes sense to me. We are bombarded with marketing and logos every second of every day: on TV, on the internet, on Billboards, even on NASCAR vehicles.

I then started ***BREW***ing. If I myself were a logo, what would I look like? And what would it stand for? Would my logo be recognizable? What about *U*? What would your logo look like? What would *U* want it to represent?

# *Brew* U

## Song Mates

I like to consider myself to be somewhat of a music buff: but choosing the right song to use as the "first dance" for my wedding has been an excruciating process.

There were so many songs out there that were "the one" until:

1.  You listened to the lyrics a bit more closely and realized that maybe that isn't the exact song you are trying to express about your future mate
2.  You realized that the tempo of the song was either too fast/too slow/or too fast then too slow all at once!
3.  You may have like the "sound of the song" or the lead singer's voice while listening to the song in the car but in an intimate setting, it just didn't have the same "feel."

Turns out, that choosing the "right song" is just like finding the "right one" to spend the rest of your life with. The relationship has to have the right rhythm, the right tempo, and be able to work no matter what life sets before you. This can be applied to anything really: jobs, friendships, and family relationships.

This got me ***BREW***ing: what song best represents *U*? What song highlights your life? What about your relationships? Your family?

# *Brew* U

## People Watching and Wondering

I am writing in a very busy coffee shop. Many people have stopped in to this shop for many reasons.

One Mother is rewarding her child with a donut for a good grade she received.
A man commented on needing a coffee to warm him up.
A group of ladies are gossiping as they sip on their java.
A police officer just remarked about having a super long shift and needing the caffeine to help him stay awake.
Two gentlemen have their laptops open and are pouring over business spreadsheets.

I am here taking advantage of the free Wi-Fi.

This curiosity over what people are doing is nothing new. I tend to **BREW** about people in their vehicles. Where are they going? Is it a fun trip? Is it a sad journey? Are they going to see friends? Is it work-related? What are they listening to?

I've also been known to gaze at people's homes and wonder what is going on inside of them. Why do I do this? I don't know. I want to say it's simply curiosity. But I wonder if there's a deeper reason. Perhaps I am afraid I am missing out on something? I honestly don't know the answer.

Do *U* ever wonder what the heck people are doing or why they do what they do? Some people call it "people watching". I call it "people wondering".

*Brew* **U**

Friendly Faces

When was the last time a stranger smiled at you? This week, I had more than 2 dozen flash me a smile, even introduced themselves to me!!

I am ***BREW***ing about this because I started a new job this week and the people that are now my co-workers are some of the nicest, most thoughtful people I have ever met! I am not sure if it's because of the profession or because they truly reflect professionalism.

Whatever the reason, many have gone out of their way to make me feel welcome, answer questions, offer insights and other helpful advice that a new co-worker would need. You may be thinking, "Wonder how long that will last?" But I will add that during the interview process, the interviewers were quick to mention that it was the people that make the company flourish. The hospitality I have received this week has really warmed my heart.

So, I will ask again, when was the last time a stranger smiled at *U*? Have *U* smiled at someone *U* don't know? It just might warm their heart.

# *Brew* U

## Your Headlines

What is the top story in your life right now? If there were a newspaper or newscast about you, what would be the big headline? Well, today's topic isn't exactly the headline other people would see, it's about the mental "head" lines you feed yourself.

I began to **BREW** about this after watching a TV show called "The Conversation." Each week features four separate celebrities (actresses, authors, fashion designers, etc.) who are asked deep-rooted questions about life, love, body image, and other things that can impact us positively or negatively. Similar to a girl's night in, the interviewer and the subject hang out on a couch or in a kitchen, sometimes with pets, and delve into deep, rich, thought-provoking subjects.

In every episode, each woman discusses how they've mentally come to terms with who they are, where they came from, what they strive to be, what lessons they've learned, and how they're applying this to their everyday lives.

As a result, each week finds me thumbing through my own thought processes or mental "head"lines. Are they valid? Where did they come from? Should they be deleted? How should they be changed?

Think about your own "head"lines. Which ones represent *U* best?

*Brew* **U**

How have yours changed over the years?

Do your "head"lines affect your actions or your beliefs about yourself?

Are your "head"lines" positive or negative?

# *Brew* U

### (Blank): It Does My Body Good

During my TV producer days, I was asked to create videos that highlight interesting facts about the body.

Did you know that by the age of 70, we'll shed 105 pounds of skin? Did you know that the body recreates bones every 10 years? Did you know that we blink around 6 million times each year?

During my research, I couldn't help but **BREW** over how our bodies are constantly working whether we notice it or not. We often tend to pay attention when something goes wrong, but how often do we pause to think (and thank) for what is going right? Because of my recent lifestyle change, I've tried to make an effort to be good to my body every single day. What have *U* done lately for the good of your body?

Fill in your blank.

_____ : It does my body good.

My answer is <u>Walking.</u> It does my body good.

# *Brew* **U**

### Happy Hour with Jesus

My husband and I burst out laughing one day when we heard the first line of a country song, "If I could have a beer with Jesus."

The artist went on to talk about how he would pick a place that wasn't crowded, listen closely to what Jesus had to say, and even pick up the tab.

As the song went on, the artist expressed his gratefulness in that Jesus loves us no matter where we are at or what we've done and will continue to do so. While the first lines of the song made us laugh with its country-twang sound and voice, it was a very happy and uplifting song. Happy hour, I thought!

Imagine meeting Jesus for happy hour? A time where there is no condemnation, no judgment, just pure unconditional love and respect. This got me **BREW**ing: if I could have a drink with Jesus, what would I want to discuss with him? What would I want to hear him say? What would I expect out of our happy hour?"

What about *U*? Can *U* picture your Happy Hour with Jesus?

# *Brew* **U**

You Scratch My Back and Wait, Keep Scratching.

Have you ever said to someone or thought, "Wow, I am so glad you have my back!"

I am *BREW*ing over this after a discussion my husband and I had about those in our lives who have supported us unconditionally. We also talked about those who have not. As he put it, "You scratch my back and just keep on scratching."

Has there ever been a time where *U* felt you were always doing the scratching? Or maybe *U* didn't scratch enough? Who's back have *U* scratched lately? And how has your back been scratched?

# *Brew* U

Score! Goal! Home Run!

The members of my immediate family are sports lovers. Not only do we like to watch games, attend games, and talk game, we even quote sports movies. Walk into our house and recite a line from a sports flick and there's a good chance my brother or my father will follow up with the next line or at least point out the title of the movie.

That said, I was excited to officially introduce my sports-loving boyfriend (now husband) to my sports-loving family as our relationship began to get serious. This event, that I dubbed "Family Bowl 2012" had some very interesting plays. Below are my x's and o's:

x) The game day, so to speak, had been building for 10+ years. Graham and I were close friends for a decade. In this situation, I was able to sit back and watch two of my favorite teams, my family and my boyfriend, meet.

o) I do not bring just anyone into the inner family circle. It's like adding a new team member to your squad. You want the best. You want the one that will gel with the rest of the players. He was all of those things – and has certainly fit in as a team player.

As I *BREW* over this, I think of my own situations where I have had to meet different players in my life. Some were great. Other turned out not to be so hot. And then there are players you meet who later turn out to be major factors in the game of life.

# *Brew* U

Do *U* remember meeting who helped *U* get ahead of the game?

# *Brew* **U**

## Motherly Advice

"Pray about it."

I will always remember these three words when I think of my Mother. Whenever I would go to her for advice, this would always be her recommendation. Sure, she would offer a few extra earthly words of insight but at the end of every Mother-daughter counselling session, she would always end it with that simple phrase.

My Mother certainly practices what she preaches. Growing up, I would see her pausing to pray before her daily devotional time. She would ask for prayer when she needed it. She would quietly pray before eating. And I know she certainly prays for those she loves each and every day, whether they are experiencing good times or bad.

Last Mother's Day, I presented my Mother with a 6 month journal. Every day, I jotted down a time, moment, or situation that made me think of her. There were childhood memories, funny Moments, or an example of how she would handle a given situation. But each and every single day, I will always remember her Motherly advice: "Pray about it."

So, as I ***BREW*** about this, I ask *U*: What is the one piece of Motherly advice that *U* will always remember? Perhaps it wasn't from a Mother, but maybe a positive female role model in your life? What "Motherly advice" will always stick with *U*?

# *Brew* **U**

## Cup o' Willpower

"Allow me to pour you a huge, steaming cup of will-power," said one of my co-workers one day. It was 6 in the morning. It was a balmy 20-something degrees and I had just finished my 2nd week of working out at 4:30am!

As I write this, I have now lived in Maine for just over one year where coffee shops, cold weather, and comfort food are the way of life for much of the year. I have watched myself "grow" into this kind of lifestyle and while I have nothing against the state itself, I am not too pleased with myself. And it has me ***BREW***ing.

Therefore, I have decided that I really need to work out in the morning. I have tried evening sessions and it doesn't work. I find myself either dreading it, not working out hard enough, or coming up with reasons to skip it. Morning is my thing. I love the early mornings. I am fresh. I truly am a morning person.

The result? I feel better. I feel back on track. Almost normal.

In order to keep up with these early morning hours, I will definitely need coffee and unlimited cups of willpower.

What about *U*? If *U* needed a huge cup of something in your life, what would it be?

# *Brew* **U**

## The Sweetest Thing

I saw the sweetest couple at a local coffee shop. They were both in their 80's and it was an early Saturday evening.

They came in and ordered two sandwiches, two cups of coffee, and a single donut that they placed in the center of their tiny table. I nonchalantly watched as they ate their sandwiches. They talked softly, laughed sweetly, and it was clear they were in love. Once they finished their sandwiches, they took the donut that was sitting in the middle of their table, split it in half, smiled at each other, ate it, and held hands afterward.

I wondered what the reason was behind the smile. Did they have some sort of a connection with this location? Was this a special occasion? An anniversary? A birthday? A guilty pleasure spot? A weekly date night? I began to **BREW** on this sweet scene and thought about some of the sweetest things in my life.

- Coffee after a workout
- Climbing into a bed with freshly washed sheets
- Getting a hug from my husband

What about *U*? What are the sweetest things in your life?

# *Brew* **U**

Your Script. Your Reality Show.

Admit it or not, I think it's safe to say that everyone reading this has watched a reality show at some point. There's a reality show catered to just about everyone and every interest. From housewives to the fashion focused, hunters to athletes, foodies to addicts, kids, animals, the list goes on and on.

And whether you watched the entire episode or just caught a glimpse of it, I'm sure you formulated some sort of opinion in your mind about what you just witnessed. Perhaps you questioned or admired the life they lead, the people they surround themselves with, or the way they treated others or were treated. After watching some of these shows, I am thankful for the reality I live; even though my reality isn't always "scripted" the way I would like it to be at all times.

I know that God is the ultimate producer of my reality series. Yet, I can't help but **BREW** over what my portrayal in my own realty show would look like to the outside world. What would viewers think of my actions? What would they think of the people in my life, my supporting cast? While it doesn't matter what other people think, my hope is that I would leave a positive impact on my viewers. I would want them to find my reality show uplifting, insightful, and filled with integrity.

Let's change the channel. Now, it's your script. It's your reality. What is your show about? What example do *U* lead? Who is your supporting cast?

# *Brew* U

## Cutting **U** Off

No bread. No sweets. 4 days. As I write this, I am in week 2 of this personal challenge.

This challenge was initiated by someone I highly admire and respect in the business and leadership world. He is urging people to identify problem foods and abstain from them for a short period of time. Not months. Not weeks. Just a few days each week.

I have watched him doing the same thing over the course of several weeks. At first, I thought "More power to him. I could never give up bread and sweets, not even for just a day!" But with each week, he has shared how his mental and physical life began to change. While excruciating for him at times, he realized how empowering it was to purposely avoid those foods. These foods were just a source of comfort to him, a distraction from feelings that needed addressed, a pause from important decisions that required answers, or in some cases, just used out of plain boredom. I couldn't help but become curious so now I am doing it.

He recently sent this message to everyone embarking on their own personal challenge: "It's good to have a program that gives you strength." I can't wait to get stronger!

Is there something *U* would like to cut out of your life? What is the first thing that comes to mind? How will *U* tackle it?

# *Brew* U

What's Your Slogan?

I'm Lovin' It. Just Do It. Let's Go Places.

Sound familiar? Many of us can name the companies behind these slogans, but have you thought about what your own individual slogan would be? We are, after all, the CEO of our own lives, so why not have one?

Slogans are creative designs for describing products, services, and most of all, promises. And just as important, it has to be memorable. Ideally, the public has to know who you are and what you can offer to make their lives work better.

For now, let's forget about the public. What are *U* most proud of about yourself? What do *U* do well? Now, bring the public back into the picture – what is it that *U* do well that can help others? Join the two together.

One of my favorite slogans of all time is from Lowe's: "Never Stop Improving." What a great line for their products and for life in general! Whenever I am feeling down, out of sorts, or even chipper, I always think of their slogan. Admittedly, I am still working on what my slogan would be. I do know that I am hard working and loyal and I am trying to merge the two. So, while I iron out my slogan, I ask you to **BREW**: what is your slogan?

*Brew* **U**

Thanks for Giving

Like so many people, I always take a moment during the Thanksgiving season to reflect on all that I am grateful for. This year, though, I found myself pausing to reflect on those people who have actually given me something extremely special: life lessons and role-modeling.

From these valuable lessons come: integrity, work ethic, drive, fairness, personal accountability, common sense, self-respect, respect of others, respect of things, just to name a few. The list really is endless. While I have had a lot of people cross my path in my very short life, it's amazing which ones have had a lasting impact and which people have been just simply passing by. In some cases, the people I thought were just a chance meeting turned out to be the people who have given me the most.

So as I ***BREW*** about this just a few days before Thanksgiving, I want to say to those who have impacted me tremendously: "Thanks for Giving." Who taught *U* some valuable life lessons? Who do *U* thank for giving?

# *Brew* U

## You've Got Male

Tis the season to recognize dear ole' Dad – or Daddy, Father, Pop, Pa; whatever the important male in your life may be called to you.

Just like many daughters, I think of my Dad fondly in many ways.

1. As my rescuer: like the time I was on the riding lawn mower on a hill and it nearly tipped over on top of me.
2. As a support system: such as financial and emotional conflicts.
3. As a confidant: he was a good shoulder to cry on.
4. As a provider: as a child, I was never without.
5. As a friend: I know I can tell my Dad anything. He may not always understand or like what I have to say, but I know I will never be judged.

As I **BREW** about these roles, I realize these don't just apply to my dad. They can be quality traits that are held by any man, whether they have children or not. I know some people who did not have close relationships with their fathers, but did receive guidance from father figure types, whom they love as if they were their father.

I challenge everyone to take a moment and remember them: male mentors, father figures, those who exude character, compassion, and moral values. Without them, I wouldn't be who I am today; and for that, I am glad. Aren't *U* glad you've got Male?

*Brew* **U**

## It Is Written

This week, I finished another chapter in my "book of life."

This was a career chapter and with it came a lot of personal elements. It had a bit of everything: heartache, frustration, victories, defeats, personal growth, and professional growth. This life chapter was definitely one of my most challenging and ultimately one of my most fulfilling.

And as I close this chapter and prepare to turn the page, I can't help but *BREW* over the chapters I have already experienced in my life. I think back on how I have tried to write the book as I want it lived out; but really it's my spiritual Author that is in control. And while my life story thus far has not always turned out the way I wanted it to be, I am grateful for what it has become.

I am still a work in progress, so I know with this next chapter in my life, I will still want to write, craft, and move the characters in such a way that will turn out to be what I think will be best. But I am trying to let go of the control, enjoy being the participant, and let the Author handle the storyline.

How are *U* handling your life story? Do *U* try and control the characters and circumstances on the page? Do *U* wish it was written differently? Are there certain things *U* had hoped for and are glad they actually didn't happen?

*Brew* **U**

## ABOUT THE AUTHOR

*Justine Shearstone is an Executive Producer, Writer, and Marketing Executive.*

*Helping people discover and achieve their true potential is her greatest passion.*

*Justine's deep-rooted conversations and experiences have led her to the beaches of Florida, the snowy mountains of Maine, and everywhere in between.*

*Justine is married to Graham and is the Stepmother of his two children, Ben and Alexis.*

www.ingramcontent.com/pod-product-compliance
Lightning Source LLC
Chambersburg PA
CBHW051233090426
42740CB00001B/8